In These Shoes We Walk

In These Shoes We Walk

MARIA WILLIAMS

Copyright

This book is a work of nonfiction. Names, characters, places, and incidents are products of the author's remembrance and have been changed for the protection of those individuals. Any resemblance to actual events, locales, or persons, living or dead, is entirely coincidental.

Manufactured & printed in the
United States of America

Publisher Maria Willams

Publisher Consultant

PRINT ISBN: 978-0-578-36239-7

Manufactured in the United States of America

DEDICATION

I dedicate this book to every grieving mother, father and sibling.

ACKNOWLEDGMENTS

I would like to thank my husband Darryl for wiping my tears away and being my protector and the love of my life.

To my children who gave me hope, love and continued joy.

To my oldest son Darrin, thanks for telling me, the day of Joshua's death, to live and believe.

To my son Kobe, you tried to save Joshua's life but God needed him more. I love you my hero!

To my son Raphael Samuel, thanks for being a hard working kid.

To my one and only daughter, Madison, thanks for being my sunshine on cloudy days.

To my mom, Earnestine Madden, thanks for instilling the word of God in me and my siblings at such a young age, and for always having my back and loving me.

To my late mother in law Jean Ethel Williams, thanks for encouraging me through this time of loss and for loving me.

To my brothers, the late Raphael, Harvey Terrell, Marcus, Joseph, Jeremy and Matthew, thank you all for being my support and army.

To my dear friend, Sister Joann Crum, thanks for praying with me late at night and even during your time of loss. Thanks for being a beautiful woman of God and a Godly role model.

To my dear seasoned mothers of God attached to my life, Mother Hall, Missionary Ivery, Missionary Diane Mitchell, Missionary Beryl and Prophetess Barbara Gaines. I love you all and thank you all for your support.

Most of all I want to thank my heavenly Father God for carrying me through the storm of my life. God has never forsaken me or let me down… to him I owe my life.

And to my personal angel Joshua Devante Williams, you are forever in my heart.

TABLE OF CONTENTS

PREFACE

Grief, n.
Hardship, suffering; a kind, or cause,
of hardship or suffering. Obsolete.

Grief is one of those terms that many are afraid to utter. Some are afraid of the category you're placed in when the world recognizes your suffering. Others tend to feel that the word itself isolates you somehow, and people suddenly become unsure of how to handle being around you. The truth is, there is no special treatment for grief. There isn't some specific way you are to handle those who are grieving than simply being supportive at whatever stage of their grief they are in.

Oxford Dictionary of English describes grief as a hardship or suffering. I'm pretty sure the person reading this book has either experienced both at some point in their lives or is experiencing them right now. We all have. The reason I'm writing this book is that I've spent some long nights wondering when I would come out of my own grievances. The thing about grief is that none of us may share the same reasons, but we are yet, a community of people who seem to reside in similar stages.

In this book, I want to share with you my personal journey of how grief happened in my life. I'll share with you the moment I realized I was in too deep and what it took to pull me out of such a dark place. More importantly, I want to share with you the different stages, how to recognize them, and scriptures to help pull you out, no matter the stage you're in. The important thing in all this is to know that you are not alone. You are not the only one fighting this battle, and there is a wealth of support here to catch you if you fall.

It has taken me years to put together the words, emotions, expressions, feelings, and the more, of where I am in my life right now and what I witnessed during my stages of grief. Everyone has a psychological or scientific perspective for the cause, but truthfully, it happens without us knowing. One moment you are smiling among family and friends and feeling like your best self. The next, you have isolated yourself from the world, and you or the people who love you can't understand why. I've been there, and I can attest to the fact that no matter where you are in your stage of grief, there is a way out.

INTRODUCTION

"Come to me, all you who are weary and burdened, and I will give you rest." – Matthew 11:28

I remember the first moment I became a mom. Seeing my child for the first time and holding him in my arms, I recognized the beauty at the moment and wanted it to last forever. I remember being concerned about my son's wellbeing. From the moment he was brought home from the hospital, I was nervous because the experience was all new to me. I had always dreamed of the moment I'd become a parent, what it would be like, and how well I would learn the ropes. I think all of us parents have experienced that. We think and obsess over the moment we will become parents and whether or not we'd be good at it.

Life doesn't give us a rule book on making it work. Instead, we are left with those before us who share the do's and don't's. They try to spare us from facing their same hardships, but I don't think you can truly ever be prepared entirely in parenthood. There will be things that happen with your children that you can't recognize. You'll be caught off guard at some of the things they do, say, etc. You will be blown away by their resilience, their wit, and more, wondering if these are the little people you brought into this world.

When I became a mom, I held my child for the first time and promised that I would do my best to protect, love, nurture, and provide for him. I repeated this same process from the first child, and for each child after.

My third born son, Joshua, is the son I prayed for, but later realized that God had other plans for him. I prayed for my son that all danger seen and unseen would never come his way. I was prepared for all that would come with raising children. Scraped knees, outgrowing clothes, terrible two's, and everything else other parents warned me of before giving birth. No matter how prepared I felt I was, nothing could have prepared me for losing my son. Joshua was my son with Godly gifts and he loved God so much. He was very intelligent. Joshua used big words and he kept a smile. That's why I was so devasted, he was my blessing from God, my prayer partner.

The most devastating moment I've experienced is the day I lost my son Joshua. He drowned in a swimming pool, and honestly, I felt so much traumatic pain from it, it took me forever to process it all. My husband and I have survived in our marriage and as parents, but there is still the absence of our son lingering over us. No one tells you how challenging days will be. How you start with blaming yourself, then quickly blaming everyone around you. They don't tell you the wave of emotion you will feel and how, if you let it, it will consume your entire life. I found myself in impossible places where I didn't think I could ever come out of. The thing about grief is that it has no respect of person. It will come in and ruin marriages, families, friendships, and more. Grief is the lack of communication and understanding. While these are traditional, dictionary-defined answers to what grief truly is, I know it to be this because I saw it for myself.

Losing my son was the hardest thing I've ever had to endure. It was harder than giving birth to each of our children. Harder than having more children after losing a child, knowing one wasn't there. I couldn't imagine giving birth after Joshua's death. It was harder than fighting for my marriage, protecting it from my grief. More complicated than supporting my husband, while we both were grieving separately. Losing a child was one of the most unimaginable experiences in my life, but through that, I learned and felt the power of God and the power of change. One day, during one of my most challenging days, God told me to not give up. He and I both knew that I was one tear away from losing my faith, hope, and love for anything in the world. See, most of us think that grief and anger is that final stage of being hurt. That is far from truth, yet I felt like that I had backslid so far, there was no possibility of return. It was until my final hour, that last glimpse of hope I had settling in the furthest part of my mind, that last moment of hearing God's voice, that I realized I needed to pull myself from the place I was falling into. One of the things I recognized is that I was beginning to lose my faith, lose my relationship with God, and that was not good.

I remember seeing my friend Joann experience the grief of losing her child, four weeks before I lost Joshua, and I couldn't have ever imagined the same thing happening to me. I saw what she went through. How she continued to pray and lay hands on others, while she was going through her own storm. I thought about her strength and just knew I was nowhere near as strong as she was. But she continued her walk with god. She continued to pray and fast and remain faithful to God's promise, and eventually, she shared that same strength and dedication with me.

Chapter One

DENIAL

"But the helper, the Holy Spirit, whom the Father will send in my name, he will teach you all things and bring to your remembrance all that I have said to you." – John 14:26

The first stage of grief is often the hardest to recognize. That is likely because for the first time, you're recognizing that the person you love dearly is no longer there. This is how I felt about my son, and for a while, I would continue to tell myself it wasn't real. Looking back, I realize that I was only hindering myself from truly grieving and moving forward. This is normal though. Denial is probably the one part of the grief process that no one can get past, unless you go through it first. You miss the laughter, the smiles, the little noises, or routines you have with those you love, so it becomes hard to recognize that those things no longer are present. They aren't there to do the things you once admired about them. They can no longer have their presence bring you comfort, because they are no longer there.

Denial is probably the hardest part of getting beyond where you are. I took it hard for a long time. I thought about the millions of things I didn't get to experience with my child. I thought about the smiles, the diaper changing, the snuggles, and the abundance of plans I had for our family, that would not come to past. No matter how hard I tried to shake those thoughts, they would continue to consume my mind and heart. Friends and family would always tell me to remember the good, but that is what made it hard to accept the loss. When we reflect on the good times, we are often stuck there. We are stuck reminiscing and dreaming about moments we once had, that we can never have again...at least not with the person we are mourning.

So how do you cope?

In these shoes, we walk together. We fight together, and we recognize that the only way to move forward is with one foot in front of the other. I found myself slowly forgetting that God is a healer of all things. The more I felt grief and denial, the more I pulled away from the Father. The first step is to talk to God. At this moment, you are struggling to understand or even grasp what has happened. This is the time to tell God what you're feeling. Put it all on the table so that you can release that pain. It is time to speak it out loud so that you and God can hear your pain and find a solution to fix it. Believe me when I say, it will be challenging. There will be long nights, late mornings, and times where you simply can't get out of bed, but the first stage in healing is to recognize the existence of your pain and ask for help.

Chapter Two

ANGER

"If the anger of the ruler rises against you, do not leave your place, for calmness will lay great offenses to rest."
– Ecclesiastes 10:4

The second stage of grief comes shortly after you have finally realized your loved one is no longer here. You've cried, you've denied their death, and on your path to finding help so that you can cope, you have realized that recognizing the loss has only made you upset. You're angry. And right now you're probably feeling like nobody understands, not even your spouse who has experienced that same trauma. This experience is common. Many people mourn the loss of a loved one and after denying their passing for so long, they become angry. As I've shared with you, at one point, I felt myself pulling away from God. I was upset with everyone. I felt like there should have been something someone was able to do to protect my child, and he would be here.

Anger is damaging to everyone. It causes you to self-destruct and then destroy everyone in your path. Think about it. If you and your spouse both experienced the same trauma, and are both going through your stages of grief, it could cause you both to pull away from one another. You are likely angry at your spouse as if they could have done anything to prevent it, while your spouse feels the same about you. I know this, because I've also felt this pain. I was so angry when I lost my child that I took that anger out on those around me, even if they were experiencing their own grief from my son's death.

So how do you cope?

The best way to cope with anger is quite similar to denial. Talk to God. Many of us stray so far from God that we can no longer hear his voice or experience his comfort. To some it may not seem like it is enough, but you have to know that this is one of the best ways to find peace. I've realized that there are not too many words "man" can say that will bring me peace or comfort. There is no amount of church service, venting to friends and family, or even yelling and screaming, that will help me release my anger about losing my child. Adopting anger in our lives only leaves us traveling down roads we are not prepared for. You cope by recognizing your pain, understanding why you are feeling it, and asking for help so that your heart and mind can feel better.

Chapter Three

BARGAINING

"The Lord is a refuge for the oppressed, a stronghold in times of trouble." – Psalm 9:9

"God I promise if you bring them back, I will do anything..." How many of you have said this? Let me be the first to say that God knows better than anyone, that you are lying. You will not do *anything*. We are human beings and have a consciousness that will prevent us from even realizing that we promised to do something that we likely won't honor. This is a form of bargaining. You're begging God to send them back so that you can do whatever he demands, but we know and God knows, that's not how it works.

Bargaining is the stage of grief where we are so hurt, we are pained, and need to compensate for the loss in any way we can. We plead with God, family, friends, or whoever will listen so that we can try to make up for our pain. Ultimately, bargaining comes because we feel as though we have failed ourselves or our loved ones. We are stuck feeling like there should have been a sign, something we could have done, but the truth is, nothing can ever prepare you for death.

So how do you cope?

You must first understand that no amount of bargaining will truly bring them back. There is no way we can do that. You can pray about it, but prayer without work of your own is dead. You have to do the work. Even though it may be extremely hard to recognize that bargaining won’t help, you have to pull yourself from doing that, because mentally, it can lead to a dark place.

Think about a few times where you did this and realize now, that nothing changed. Things only got progressively worse, and it likely left you in a place of depression. You don’t’ want to do this to yourself. When we are in the thick of things, it can often be hard to recognize what’s really happening, but you have to remember that some things in life happen for a reason. Of course we don’t understand why and may never truly get all the answers, but all of our places in this life are seasonal.

Chapter Four

DEPRESSION

"Lord my God, I called to you for help and you healed me." – Psalm 30:2

Everyone has experienced depression at one time or another, in their lives. The problem is, depression from grief is often hard to shake. The brutal truth is that not everyone is capable of pulling themselves out of depression. I can attest that it was extremely hard for me. I thought that I would find some relief. I went through the denial of losing my son. I remember the anger I held towards everyone. I remember bargaining with God and my husband. Pleading to them both, asking for different things, and willing to sacrifice my own life to have my child back. It was long after that I realized all of those moments made me depressed in some way. I began to lay in bed for days, not wanting to get out. I didn't want to bathe, eat, or even talk to anyone. I didn't want to watch TV or do any of the things I enjoyed. I had found myself deeply rooted in my depression that it was far beyond my control.

So how do you cope?

The best way to cope is through doing something that brings you comfort. I have a friend who lost her oldest brother. She was devastated from his passing, because they were extremely close. While there was a huge age difference between the two, her 30 and him 62, they carried on like they were the same age. Both are gemini's and always celebrated their birthdays together. When he passed away this past january, she found herself in the worst depression she'd experienced before. She struggled for months, not wanting to get out of bed, randomly crying, and trying to work nonstop to get through it or not deal with it at all. She later realized it was time to really pull herself together, or she would be depressed for a while.

I am happy to say that my friend was able to pull herself out of her depression, but in a way that was unique to her. She would draw digital drawings of her brother throughout the stages of her life. It allowed her to connect with him from his childhood to adulthood through her illustrations. It brought her peace.

My point in all this is that, it may seem super easy to simply say "pray about it," so I won't say that. Of course, pray for comfort and understanding, but do something that puts you in the same space as the person you lost. Drink their favorite beverage, prepare a meal they once enjoyed. Do something that takes you to a time you both shared and remember from a place of love. Watch their favorite cartoons or movies.

Chapter Five

ACCEPTANCE

"Weeping may endure for a night but joy comes in the morning." – Psalm 30:5

It has taken you some time, but you made it. You have advanced in your healing, enough to accept that what has happened is already done, and there is nothing more to do than move forward. As you may have noticed, it was hard getting here. You had to go through some trials and tribulations, but you made it. It's natural. We find ourselves holding on so closely to things that are no longer existent in our lives, that we forget to continue living. That goes for the loss of our loved ones too. You don't have to let go of their memories or the love you have for them, but in order for them to rest, you have to let them go. That's what I've learned.

I'm only speaking on this because I experienced it first hand. I know what it's like. I know your pain, I've seen it all too well. I remember getting the phone call about my baby boy. I remember the many nights I cried and just wanted to trade my life for his. It's the kind of pain I would never wish on anyone. That's why I wrote this book. I want to help you heal, but I also want you to know that the journey you're embracing is natural and that you're not alone. In these Shoes We Walk, hand in hand, and in prayer, so that we all find peace in our grief.

CONCLUSION

In these Shoes We Walk

"Do you not know? Have you not heard? The Lord is the everlasting God, the Creator of the ends of the earth. He will not grow tired or weary, and his understanding no one can fathom. He gives strength to the weary and increases the power of the weak. Even youths grow tired and weary, and young men stumble and fall; but those who hope in the Lord will renew their strength. They will soar on wings like eagles; they will run and not grow weary, they will walk and not be faint." – **Isaiah 40:18-31**

There are three intentions that I want to leave with you. We should intentionally have an understanding and walk in:

- Faith
- Love
- Hope

When I think of **faith**, I can't help but to think of how much I trust God. I know that he knows my endurance level better than anyone, so I trust him to heal me even when things that are done to hurt me, he already knows about. I've heard so much over time that God will never put more on you than you can bear, but we always seem to question him when things get hard. Just because we feel that we are at our peak of pain, it doesn't mean that God feels that way. He's an all knowing God, so he knows that we will get through whatever pain we are feeling. The real test is to see how faithful we will continue to be, even at our darkest moments.

God's **love** is also something deeper than our imagination. God loves us so much that he will do everything he can to take care of us. Sometimes that can mean taking something we love or allowing us to only have it for a season. That can include family. I know women who lost their husbands during the pandemic and were devastated. Those same women felt that their lives would never move forward and while they are holding on to the memories they have left, they have found some peace within the storm. God's love is enough to comfort us during a storm, just like he's done for the women who lost their husbands. His love is so faithful at one point, I wondered how I was going to move forward and God showed me the way. I kept my mind on God and his promise. "Thou will keep thou mind in perfect peace who mind is stayed on thee." – Isaiah 26:3

Because of our faith and God's love, we can have **hope** for a better tomorrow. Our hope outweighs all of the pain we have experienced because we know that there is something better. There will be a day where we don't cry as much. There will be a way we can finally reconnect with our spouse, after rejecting their love and affection for so long. There will be a time where we can gather with family and share laughter again, without the pain of losing someone isn't holding us back from living our lives. We have hope that God will heal us in ways unimaginable and we will be able to look back and be grateful for the journey ahead. It seems so far from our current reach, but through it all, there will be a time where we can overcome everything we've held on to.

I have faith in you, that you will recognize that you are not walking along. That you will see me reaching my hand out to comfort you on this journey and that the tools I've provided in this book will help you continue to put one foot in front of the other. I want to leave you with one final scripture, it is one that has kept me along the way.

"Fear not, for I am with you; be not dismayed, for I am your God. I will strengthen you, yes, I will help you, I will uphold you with my righteous right hand." – Isaiah 41:10

ABOUT THE AUTHOR

Maria Williams is a wife, a mother, a child of God, an author, a business owner she owns Chosen People Home Health Agency, a service that provides care for the geriatric and veteran community. She also owns Joshua's Place Care Home is a service that provides housing for the veterans and geriatric community. Caring for others is her passion. For Booking, Speaking, and Live readings contact Maria's office at www.iamafaithwalker.com

www.ingramcontent.com/pod-product-compliance
Lightning Source LLC
Chambersburg PA
CBHW030512100426
42813CB00001B/13
9780578362397